THE MIND READER'S HANDBOOK

Step-by-Step Guide to Analyzing and Influencing Human Behavior

Judy Theodorah

TABLE OF CONTENT

INTRODUCTION

The Mind Reader's Handbook: Step by Step Guide to Analyzing and Influencing Human Behavior is a stunning and keen book that dives into the fascinating universe of getting a handle on the intricacies of human approach to acting.

Mind perusing could seem like something out of a science fiction film, but this book reveals the science behind it. It makes sense of that perceptiveness, in this book, isn't connected to scrutinizing certifiable contemplations, yet rather sorting out the prompts, models, and signs that people accidentally reveal through their non-verbal correspondence, microexpressions, and verbal signs.

This pivotal book, The Mind Reader's Handbook, can possibly totally change your life. You can involve the procedures and bits of knowledge in this book to all the more likely grasp the human brain, construct more grounded connections, and understand your maximum capacity.

This handbook's accentuation on further developing your relational abilities is quite possibly of its most significant element. Having the option to really peruse individuals' contemplations and feelings can give you a gigantic benefit in different circumstances.

Correspondence is a fundamental piece of our day to day routines. The Mind Reader's Handbook unravels the privileged insights of non-verbal signs, non-verbal correspondence, and looks, allowing you to unequivocally interpret and grasp what others are truly thinking and feeling. This is particularly profitable in capable settings, for instance, planned representative gatherings, talks, or any situation where practical correspondence is huge.

Moreover, the Mind Reader's Handbook gives valuable experiences into the meaning of the capacity to appreciate anyone on a deeper level and sympathy. By sorting out some way to figure people's contemplations and sentiments, you can cultivate a more significant sensation of empathy, engaging you to create more grounded affiliations and foster more critical associations. Understanding others on a more significant level can help you with investigating conflicts, manage difficult situations, and ultimately work on the idea of your associations with others.

Past additional fostering your social capacities, the Visionary's Handbook also jumps into the possibility of care. You can recognize restrictive convictions, overcome pessimistic examples, and implement positive improvements in your day-to-day life by gaining a greater understanding of your own thoughts and feelings. The handbook provides a variety of activities and methods that can help you investigate your own psyche and cultivate identity mindfulness that is more grounded.

The Mind Reader's Handbook hangs out in alternate ways because of its accentuation on self-improvement and development. This handbook goes past the surface level of perceptiveness and bounces significant into the cerebrum science behind human approach to acting. You can gain significant insight into your own inspirations and discover better methods for achieving your goals by comprehending the hidden rules that drive our thoughts and actions.

The Handbook isn't just a manual for sorting out others; It can assist you with changing what your identity is. It empowers you to exploit your own actual limit, become more careful, and cultivate an expanded level of the ability to figure out individuals on a significant level. The methods and pieces of information presented in this handbook might conceivably change how you team up with others, investigate through life's hardships, and finally make a truly fulfilling and productive life.

The Mind Reader's Handbook is major areas of strength for a that can thoroughly completely change you. Whether you're attempting to additionally foster your social capacities, cultivate more grounded associations, or open your own actual limit, this handbook gives the mechanical assemblies and data to help you with achieving your goals. In case you're ready to expect control over your life, gain a more significant perception of others, and show up at new degrees of mindfulness, then, the Visionary's Handbook is a by and large must-scrutinize. Get ready to embark on a ground-breaking journey that will forever alter your perspective and inspire you to become the best version of yourself.

CHAPTER 1

THE SUPPORTING OF PERCEPTIVENESS

1.1. The science behind mind examining

Mind examining, oftentimes saw as a grand limit, has hypnotized individuals for a seriously significant time-frame. Having the choice to grasp someone's inside perspectives, fears, or needs with no verbal correspondence gives off an impression of being for all intents and purposes supernatural. In any case, late headways in neuroscience and brain research have revealed insight into the study of telepathy, uncovering the basic components that empower us to grasp and decipher the considerations of others and scattering the bewilderment that encompasses the peculiarity.

We should examine two fundamental regions to grasp the mind reading science: compassion and mirror neurons. Sympathy is the ability to appreciate and examine the contemplations of others. It incorporates seeing sentiments as well as having the choice to see and sort out the considerations and points behind them. Reflect neurons, of course, are explicit cells in the frontal cortex that fire both when a singular plays out an action and when they notice someone else playing out a comparative movement. These mirror neurons accept a basic part by they way we understand and interpret the exercises, assumptions, and sensations of others.

Reflect neurons was first tracked down by Italian neuroscientist Giacomo Rizzolatti and his gathering during the 1990s. They found that specific neurons in the premotor and parietal cortex of macaque monkeys enacted not just when the actual monkeys played out a specific activity yet additionally when they noticed other monkeys or people playing out a similar activity. These mirror neurons make a cerebrum reflecting system that licenses individuals to fathom and duplicate the exercises they notice.

This reflecting structure isn't limited to straightforward exercises anyway connects with sentiments as well. For example, when we see someone smiling, our mirror neurons fire, making a propagation of the saw lead as far as we could tell. Without really grinning, we can appreciate and encounter bliss through this brain recreation. Basically, when we see someone in torture, our mirror neurons make a diversion of that experience, engaging us to connect with their wretchedness.

The job of mirror neurons in appreciating the considerations and expectations of others has been additionally upheld by late fMRI-based examinations. These examinations have uncovered that when individuals notice someone playing out an action, not at all do their mirror neurons fire, but unambiguous region of the brain obligated for point understanding and mentalizing furthermore become dynamic. This suggests that reflect neurons, close by other frontal cortex areas, participate to help us with sorting out the thoughts and objectives of others.

Despite the way that reflect neurons expect a basic part at the highest point of the need list scrutinizing, it is fundamental for observe that perceptiveness is surely not a cautious science. It is influenced by an extent of components, including social establishment, individual differences, and setting. Two individuals with different experiences and social establishments could unravel a comparable action or feeling surprisingly. Also, the precision of mind reading can in like manner be affected by short lived factors like shortcoming, stress, or interference.

No matter what these hardships, analysts have made colossal progress in making methods to measure and grasp mind scrutinizing. One such method is commonsense close infrared spectroscopy (fNIRS), which evaluations changes in blood oxygenation in the brain to perceive regions related with mentalizing and sorting out points. fNIRS has shown ensure in helping researchers with unraveling the convoluted association of frontal cortex regions drew in with mind scrutinizing.

Additionally, movements in man-caused awareness and artificial intelligence to have allowed specialists to cultivate estimations that can predict and unravel human contemplations and sentiments considering frontal cortex activity. By looking at plans in fMRI data, these estimations can disentangle the mental states and assumptions for individuals fairly. But these methods are still in their beginning, they hold remarkable potential for empowering appreciation we could decipher mind scrutinizing.

Compassion and mirror neurons are the cerebrums behind the study of mind examining. Compassion and the reflecting framework made by reflect neurons are the groundworks of our ability to understand and decipher the considerations and expectations of others. While mind scrutinizing is absolutely not an optimal science and is affected by various factors, advancing investigation and types of progress in neuroscience and development are conveying us nearer to opening the secrets of this capacity to enamor. By understanding the science behind mind examining, we could procure further encounters into human appreciation and prepare for up to this point unfathomable enhancements in fields like cerebrum examination, neuroscience, and mechanized thinking.

1.2 Cultivating solid areas

Cultivating solid areas for an is unquestionably not a natural gift that two or three fortunate individuals have; an ability can be created and refined after some time. Sense is commonly depicted as a feeling or an instinct that guides us through life's weaknesses, helping us with making better decisions and investigate our course through the muddled catch of choices.

With practically no consistent thinking or proof to help it, instinct is much of the time compared with a significant feeling of knowing. It is that subtle voice inside us that mumbles the right method for following or alerts us of anticipated gambles. Regardless, cultivating serious solid areas for a requires working on unequivocal capacities and practices in our standard schedules.

The most imperative move towards encouraging solid areas for an is to account for serenity and quietness. In our speedy moving, development driven world, becoming consumed by outside upheaval and interruptions is straightforward. Getting a charge out of respites from consistent energy and making quiet previews of reflection allows our intuition to surface and be heard. Reflection, care, and significant breathing exercises can help us with calming our minds and set aside that genuinely important room for impulse to thrive. Focusing on our body is another huge piece of making intuition. Our body has an inborn information that habitually gives critical information to us before our aware mind does. Zeroing in on genuine sensations, sentiments, and subtle changes can offer hints and pieces of information that can coordinate our dynamic connection. With regards to fostering serious areas of strength for a, believing our substantial sensations and hunches can be a strong partner.

Seeing models and synchronicities in our lives can in like manner assist with working on our inherent abilities. Acknowledgment of significant associations or occurrences that might seem irrelevant at first is regularly connected to instinct. By successfully seeing and reflecting upon these models, we can begin to exploit the more significant appreciation and encounters that our intuition gives.

Practicing dynamic interest and generosity is essential for supporting impulse. Pushing toward presence with a sensation of wonder and receptivity licenses us to see past the surface level and explore the mystery layers of this present reality. We increment our mindfulness and become more open to additional opportunities when we ask, research, and look for information. This straightforwardness empowers our impulse as it urges us to ponder all perspectives and expected results before choosing.

Developing serious areas of fortitude for a moreover requires self-trust and fostering a sensation of internal knowing. Second guessing ourselves and searching for outside endorsement can cloud our intuition and steer us from our genuine way. By sorting out some way to believe our own judgment and nature, we encourage a more significant care as well as draw in ourselves to go with decisions considering our inward understanding.

Finally, it is essential to observe that cultivating solid areas for an is a consistent cycle that requires industriousness and practice. There may be times when our impulse seems to bomb us or when we question its authenticity. Regardless, with unsurprising effort and commitment, our sense will form further and transform into a coordinating power in our lives. Cultivating solid areas for a will be a mastery that can be created and refined through various practices and mindset shifts. We can take advantage of our instinct and open its boundless potential by making tranquility, paying attention to our body, noticing designs, staying inquisitive, creating self-trust, and rehearsing persistence. Embracing our nature grants us to make extra instructed decisions, investigate life's weaknesses effectively, and in the long run continue with a truly fulfilling and trustworthy life.

1.3 Structure Compassion and The capacity to understand people on a deeper level

Compassion and the capacity to understand people on a profound level are two urgent abilities that assume a critical part in our proficient development. These abilities permit us to comprehend and associate with others, settle on better choices, and explore different social collaborations smartly and humanely. Building compassion and the capacity to understand people at their core is a deep-rooted process that requires self-reflection, practice, and ceaseless learning. we will jump into the meaning of these capacities and examine fruitful approaches to creating them.

Sympathy is the ability to grasp and discuss the contemplations of another person. It entails imagining another person's point of view, listening with an open mind, and recognizing their emotions without judging. Making empathy licenses us to develop strong associations, work on our social capacities, and make a more exhaustive and thoughtful culture.

The capacity to appreciate anyone on a profound level, then again, alludes to the capacity to recognize, comprehend, and deal with our feelings and the feelings of others. It includes perceiving and controlling our sentiments, as well as being delicate to the feelings of everyone around us. The capacity to understand people at their core empowers us to impart, handle clashes with effortlessness, and fabricate better connections.

Presently, we should investigate a few compelling procedures to fabricate compassion and the capacity to understand people on a deeper level:

1. **Undivided attention:** Quite possibly the main move toward building compassion is undivided attention. This implies concentrating on the speaker, keeping away from interruptions, and grasping their viewpoint. To accurately comprehend the speaker's feelings, it involves paraphrasing, asking open-ended questions, and seeking clarification.

2. **Practice Viewpoint Taking**: Empathy requires us to put ourselves in another person's shoes and view the world from their perspective. To foster this expertise, we can participate in context-taking activities, for example, envisioning ourselves in various circumstances or jobs, perusing assorted writing, or electing to work with people from various foundations.

3. **Develop Mindfulness:** The capacity to understand people on a profound level beginnings with mindfulness. Grasping our feelings, assets, shortcomings, and triggers permits us to all the more likely figure out others.

Rehearsing care, journaling, and considering our encounters can help in creating mindfulness and the ability to appreciate anyone on a profound level.

4. **Approve Feelings:** Approval is a useful asset in building sympathy. At the point when somebody communicates their feelings to us, it is fundamental to recognize and approve their sentiments. It is not necessary to agree with the feelings of others to validate them; rather, it implies showing compassion and figuring out their viewpoint.

5. **Practicing emotional control:** The capacity to appreciate individuals on a deeper level includes dealing with our feelings. This incorporates perceiving our triggers, rehearsing poise, and tracking down solid ways of adapting to pressure and gloomy feelings. Taking part in exercises like reflection, profound breathing activities, or looking for help from believed people can help in creating close-to-home guideline abilities.

6. **Gain according to Assorted Viewpoints:** It is essential to expose ourselves to diverse perspectives and experiences to develop empathy and emotional intelligence. This should be possible by effectively searching out various perspectives, taking part in open conversations, or finding out about various societies and foundations. We grow in our comprehension and capacity for empathy the more we learn from other people.

7. **Assemble Connections**: Significant associations with others give important chances to rehearse sympathy and the capacity to appreciate anyone on a profound level. These abilities can develop through deep conversations, genuine care and compassion, and active support of others' emotional journeys.

8. **Look for Input:** Criticism from believed people can assist us with recognizing vulnerable sides and regions for development in our sympathy and the capacity to appreciate anyone at their core abilities. Inviting productive analysis and doing whatever it may take to roll out certain improvements can speed up our development and advancement around there.

Building sympathy and the ability to understand individuals at their core is critical for individual and expert development. By effectively rehearsing undivided attention, viewpoint taking, mindfulness, close-to-home guidelines, and looking for different encounters, we can improve how we might interpret others, deal with our feelings really, and construct significant associations. The excursion towards building compassion and the capacity to understand people on a profound level is a long-lasting undertaking, yet the advantages are broad - both for us and for the general public we live in.

CHAPTER 2

SKILLS IN OBSERVATION

2.1 Sharpening Your Senses: Upgrading Your Discernment and Mindfulness

Our faculties are the entryways to our general surroundings. They permit us to encounter and decipher the data that encompasses us. Whether it's the flavor of a scrumptious feast, the hint of a friend or family member, seeing a wonderful nightfall, the sound of music, or the fragrance of a sprouting blossom, our faculties assume a significant part in molding our regular encounters. Fortunately, we can hone our faculties and improve our insight and mindfulness. In this section, we will investigate different ways of achieving this and the advantages that accompany it.

The Significance of Honing Your Faculties:

Having the option to completely draw in and value our faculties carries various advantages to our lives. At the point when we hone our faculties, we increase our consciousness of the current second, prompting a more profound and more extravagant experience of life. By preparing our faculties to be more open, we can all the more likely value the little delights and joys that frequently slip through the cracks in our bustling lives. Also, honing our faculties can upgrade our general prosperity, work on mental capability, and, surprisingly, cultivate innovativeness.

Systems for Honing Your Faculties:

1. **Care and Contemplation:** Practicing mindfulness and meditation

effectively improves sensory perception. By preparing your psyche to be completely present at the time, you can notice your general surroundings with more prominent lucidity and profundity. Focusing on one sense at a time, such as the sensation of your breath or the sound of a single note in music, is a good place to start. As you practice, step by step extend your attention to incorporate every one of your faculties, permitting you to drench yourself right now completely.

2. **Participate in Tactile Exercises:** It is possible to significantly sharpen your senses by participating in activities that stimulate them. Consider taking up a side interest like photography, painting, or cooking, which permits you to work on focusing on the subtleties of variety, surface, and taste. Encountering nature through climbing, cultivating, or birdwatching can likewise stir your faculties to the magnificence and multifaceted design of the normal world.

3. **Attempt New Preferences and Flavors:** Our feeling of taste is frequently disregarded, as we will generally adhere to natural and unsurprising flavors. Nonetheless, growing your culinary skylines and investigating new preferences can stir your taste buds and improve your feeling of taste. Visit new cafés, explore different avenues regarding various cooking styles, and attempt intriguing and new food sources. Focus on the flavors, surfaces, and mixes, and relish each chomp.

4. **Sensory Activities:** Participating in unambiguous activities customized for each sense can likewise assist with honing them. Practice carefully observing and describing your surroundings, for instance, to improve your vision. Notice the tones, shapes, and examples of items you experience. Additionally, to improve your feeling of touch, attempt various surfaces and materials, similar to silk, sand, or velvet, and spotlight the sensations they summon.

5. **Wipe out Interruptions:** Our faculties can without much of a stretch become dulled by consistent openness to interruptions like innovation and commotion. To upgrade your tangible discernment, really try to consistently

disengage from electronic gadgets. Invest energy in calm conditions, away from the consistent upgrades of day-to-day existence. This will permit your faculties to reset and turn out to be more sensitive to the unpretentious subtleties of your general surroundings.

The Advantages of Honing Your Faculties:

1. **Elevated Mindfulness**: At the point when our faculties are sharp, we become more receptive to our environmental elements, seeing both the self-evident and the unobtrusive subtleties that frequently slip by everyone's notice. This elevated mindfulness permits us to connect all the more completely with the current second, prompting a more prominent feeling of connectedness, bliss, and appreciation.

2. **Worked on Mental Capability:** Through deliberate, focused observation, you can also improve your cognitive function by sharpening your senses. Via preparing your psyche to be more mindful, you can work on your memory, fixation, and generally speaking smartness.

3. **Increased Emotional Bonding:** At the point when our faculties are increased, we can encounter feelings all the more with great intensity. Honing our faculties can develop our close-to-home association with the world and with other people, permitting us to encounter more significant snapshots of happiness, love, and sympathy.

4. **Expanded Innovativeness:** Improving our tangible discernment additionally sustains our inventive capacities. By being more perceptive of our general surroundings, we can draw motivation from the magnificence of nature, the complicated associations of individuals, and the extravagance of our current circumstances. This, thus, can fuel our creative minds and upgrade our imaginative articulation.

Honing our faculties is a deep-rooted venture that requires commitment, care, and practice. By tuning into the different features of our faculties, we open the potential for a more energetic and significant experience of life.

Each moment becomes an opportunity for deeper connection and appreciation, from the taste of food to the touch of a loved one. Therefore, let's set out on this journey to sharpen our senses and allow ourselves to be completely present, aware, and alive in the world around us.

2.2 Grasping Non-verbal Correspondence

Non-verbal correspondence is a fundamental part of human connection that frequently slips through the cracks or assumes a lower priority than verbal correspondence. Be that as it may, the effect of nonverbal prompts ought to be acknowledged with a sober mind as they can fundamentally impact how we comprehend and decipher messages.

What is Nonverbal Correspondence?

Nonverbal correspondence alludes to the trading of data through non-phonetic and non-composed implies. It includes signals, looks, body developments, stances, eye-to-eye connection, contact, and, surprisingly, the utilization of actual space. Not at all like verbal correspondence, which utilizes words and language, nonverbal correspondence depends on visual and hearable signs to convey meaning.

The Importance of Nonverbal Communication In interpersonal interactions, nonverbal communication is crucial for understanding and interpreting messages and can sometimes be more potent and accurate than spoken words. The following are a couple of justifications for why understanding nonverbal correspondence is fundamental:

1. **Improving Comprehension:** Nonverbal signs give extra setting and importance to verbal correspondence. They can explain or go against the verbally expressed words, empowering us to all the more likely figure out the speaker's actual aims or feelings.

2. **Communicating Feelings:** Nonverbal signs are in many cases more

dependable in communicating feelings precisely. Looks, manner of speaking, and non-verbal communication can give us an understanding of somebody's sentiments, paying little heed to what they say.

3. **Building Connections:** Nonverbal communication aids in the development of trust and rapport in relationships. Understanding and properly answering nonverbal prompts can assist in structuring more grounded associations with others and improve correspondence.

4. **Disparities in culture:** Nonverbal correspondence designs change across societies, and monitoring these distinctions can assist with keeping away from errors and encourage powerful culturally diverse correspondence.

Sorts of Nonverbal Correspondence

1. **Non-verbal communication**: A lot of information can be conveyed through gestures, postures, and facial expressions. Crossed arms, for instance, may signify defensiveness, whereas relaxed posture, open palms, and acceptance may.

2. **Looks**: The face is unquestionably expressive and can convey different feelings like satisfaction, shock, outrage, bitterness, and dread. Grins, caused by a stir, or wrinkled temples can essentially influence the understanding of a message.

3. **Eye-to-eye connection**: How individuals use eye-to-eye connection can show their degree of interest, commitment, or even trickery. Keeping in touch during a discussion shows mindfulness and regard while staying away from eye-to-eye connection could recommend uneasiness or deceitfulness.

4. **Manner of speaking:** The pitch, volume, and enunciation in one's voice can convey a scope of feelings or perspectives. The same words can sound more inviting when delivered in a friendly and warm tone, whereas a harsh and cold tone can elicit hostility or distance.

5. **Proxemics**: Proxemics alludes to the investigation of individual space and how individuals use it to impart. The distance between people during a discussion can convey various degrees of closeness, convention, or

predominance.

6. **Touch**: Contact can be a strong method for imparting different feelings and expectations. A consoling embrace or a congratulatory gesture can convey sympathy and backing, while a forceful or limited crossing contact can bring out uneasiness or even trepidation.

Enhancing Your Understanding of Nonverbal Communication Consider the Following Advice to Improve Your Skills in Nonverbal Communication:

1. **Observe**: Observe nonverbal cues in various social settings. Notice individuals' non-verbal communication, looks, and signals to acquire knowledge of their correspondence style and feelings.

2. **Develop empathy:** Put yourself in the shoes of the other person and try to comprehend the feelings they might be going through based on what they don't say. This can assist you with creating sympathy and answering suitably.

3. **Be Aware of Your Nonverbal Correspondence:** Know about the signs you are sending through your non-verbal communication, looks, and manner of speaking. Adjust your nonverbal prompts to your expected message to keep away from contradicting messages.

4. **Find out about Social Contrasts**: Get to know nonverbal correspondence designs in various societies to successfully explore culturally diverse connections more. Keep away from suppositions and generalizations by exploring and posing inquiries while speaking with people from assorted foundations.

5. **Look for Input:** Ask confided-in people, like companions, tutors, or associates, for criticism of your nonverbal relational abilities. They can give significant experiences and assist you with recognizing regions for development.

Nonverbal correspondence is a vital piece of human collaboration that can essentially influence how messages are perceived and deciphered. By being aware of nonverbal prompts and working on how we might interpret them, we can upgrade our relational abilities, construct more grounded connections, and explore collaborations all the more successfully.

2.3. Examining looks and non-verbal communication

Examining looks and non-verbal communication is a vital expertise that can give significant bits of knowledge into an individual's viewpoints, sentiments, and goals. People are intrinsically friendly creatures, continually trading nonverbal signals through their looks, motions, and stances. These nonverbal prompts frequently convey feelings, mentalities, and secret expectations that may not be expressly imparted through words. By figuring out how to decipher and investigate these signs, one can acquire a more profound comprehension of relational elements, further develop relational abilities, and even recognize duplicity.

Looks are viewed as the main part of the nonverbal correspondence, as they give prompt and visual data about an individual's close-to-home state. As indicated by the earth-shattering exploration of Dr. Paul Ekman, seven essential widespread feelings can be distinguished through looks: joy, sorrow, resentment, fear, surprise, disgust, and contempt These feelings are communicated through a mix of muscle developments around the eyes, mouth, and different region of the face.

Dissecting looks includes noticing and deciphering these developments and their power. For instance, a crow's feet around the eyes, a wider smile, and raised cheeks are all signs of happiness, while a downturned mouth, droopy eyelids, and a furrowed brow are signs of sadness. Understanding these viewable prompts can help with checking an individual's close-to-home state, assisting with building compatibility and sympathy, or in any event, flagging when somebody is in trouble and may need support.

Non-verbal communication, then again, envelops a more extensive range of nonverbal prompts, including motions, stances, and developments. Body language, in contrast to facial expressions, is not limited to a single set of cues and can be influenced by a person's personality and culture. By the by, there are sure all-inclusive non-verbal communication signs that can uncover an individual's certainty, interest, solace, or uneasiness.

For example, an open and loosened-up act, with arms uncrossed and legs somewhat separated, shows an individual's transparency and commitment. Going against the norm, crossing arms and legs, slumping, or squirming can flag preventiveness, lack of engagement, or distress. Besides, the heading of an individual's look can likewise uncover their contemplations or expectations. Depending on the situation, avoiding eye contact may indicate dishonesty, while maintaining eye contact may indicate interest or aggression.

Breaking down non-verbal communication includes noticing these signals in harmoniousness with other nonverbal and verbal ways of behaving. For instance, assuming somebody is gesturing their head in arrangement while saying "no," their non-verbal communication goes against their current verbal message, demonstrating likely double-dealing or uneasiness with the point. Similarly, observing one another's posture or gestures and mirroring them can help establish rapport and a sense of connection.

However, it is essential to keep in mind that cultural, individual, and situational considerations should all be taken into account when interpreting facial expressions and body language. Social standards and individual mannerisms can impact how individuals put themselves out there nonverbally, and not all signals or developments have widespread implications. It is pivotal to be aware of these social distinctions and perceive that nonverbal signs ought to be deciphered inside their separate settings.

Breaking down looks and non-verbal communication isn't restricted to up close and personal connections alone. With progressions in innovation, the utilization of facial acknowledgment programming and video examination has become progressively pervasive. This innovation can help with deciphering looks and non-verbal communication progressively, empowering applications in fields, for example, brain science, statistical surveying, and security.

In brain science, the examination of looks and non-verbal communication is utilized in different fields, including treatment, lie identification, and feeling acknowledgment. Specialists can recognize close-to-home states and check the advancement of their clients by noticing their nonverbal signs during meetings. Lie recognition methods, for example, the Facial Activity Coding Framework (FACS), dissect microexpressions and unobtrusive developments to precisely distinguish misdirection. Feeling acknowledgment programming is currently being created to help people with mental imbalance range problems recognize and figure out feelings through facial signals.

Analyzing people's body language and facial expressions can be a useful tool in advertising and market research. By observing members' looks while they view ads or collaborate with items, scientists can acquire a superior comprehension of close-to-home commitment and buy purpose. Companies can use this data to improve their marketing campaigns and refine their marketing strategies.

Security is another field where investigating looks and non-verbal communication have viable applications. Noticing people's conduct in high-stress circumstances, security faculty can evaluate likely dangers or dubious exercises. Additionally, facial recognition software can assist with individual identification for security purposes, such as access control systems or airports.

Examining looks and non-verbal communication is a significant ability that can upgrade relational correspondence, give further experiences into feelings and goals, and work on understanding across societies. By learning and rehearsing the craft of translation, one can foster a superior comprehension of nonverbal prompts, prompting more powerful correspondence, further developed connections, and an increased capacity to explore social cooperation.

JUDY THEODORAH

CHAPTER 3

MENTAL PROFILING

3.1 Distinguishing examples of conduct

Distinguishing examples of conduct is a captivating part of both brain research and daily existence. People are predictable animals, and we frequently show steady examples in our viewpoints, feelings, and activities. Perceiving these examples can offer important bits of knowledge about somebody's personality, inspirations, and goals. It can likewise assist us with understanding ourselves better and coming to informed conclusions about our way of behaving.

Examples of conduct can appear in different ways and can be seen in various settings. They should be visible in private connections, proficient conditions, social communications, or even in our inner contemplations and feelings. A few normal examples of conduct incorporate confidence or inactivity, compulsiveness, tarrying, human satisfaction, self-destructive behavior, or an inclination to keep away from struggle. By focusing on these examples, we can acquire a more profound comprehension of ourselves as well as other people.

One compelling method for recognizing examples of conduct is through cautious perception. We can begin to notice recurring themes or tendencies by being conscious of someone's actions, words, and body language. For instance, an individual who reliably hinders others during discussions might uncover an example of consideration chasing or an absence of sympathy. Likewise, somebody who reliably takes on more work than they can deal with may show an example of overcommitment or a feeling of dread toward saying no.

Another supportive methodology is to look at the outcomes of specific ways of behaving. Individuals frequently rehash activities that bring them wanted results or give a feeling of solace or security. For instance, a pattern of seeking validation or avoiding feelings of uncertainty may be present in a person who constantly seeks reassurance from others. By understanding the hidden inspirations and prizes related to a way of behaving, we can acquire knowledge into why it perseveres.

Also, considering previous encounters can uncover examples of conduct that may not be quickly obvious. Glancing back at critical occasions or repeating topics in our lives can feature designs that we might have recently disregarded. For example, steady work disappointment or bombed connections might show an example of self-destructive behavior or a feeling of dread toward closeness.

Mental appraisals and character tests can likewise be instrumental in distinguishing examples of conduct. These evaluations give a system for figuring out various character qualities and propensities. They can give us valuable insights into how we see the world, get along with other people, and deal with different situations. By perceiving our examples of conduct through these evaluations, we can move toward self-improvement and personal development.

Moreover, looking for criticism from others can assist with distinguishing examples of conduct that we probably won't know about ourselves. Confided-in companions, relatives, or even experts can express true impressions and bits of knowledge. Perspectives from other people can help us see patterns or blind spots that we may not be aware of.

When examples of conduct have been recognized, considering their potential impact is fundamental. A few examples might be gainful and lead to positive results, while others might be hurtful or counterproductive. Understanding these examples enables us to make cognizant decisions about our activities and reactions, permitting us to break negative cycles and develop better ways of behaving.

Recognizing examples of conduct is an imperative device for self-awareness, grasping others, and exploring social communications. We can identify recurring themes and tendencies in both ourselves and those around us through careful observation, reflection, investigation of consequences, psychological assessments, and feedback from others. By tackling this mindfulness, we can go with informed choices and foster better examples of conduct, prompting more noteworthy individual joy and achievement.

3.2 Perceiving Character Qualities

Character qualities assume a significant part in how people see and explore their general surroundings. These characteristics, which are a mix of hereditary and natural variables, impact different parts of an individual's way of behaving, considerations, and feelings.

Understanding and perceiving character attributes assists in self-disclosure as well as in working with bettering connections, settling on informed professional decisions, and tending to clashes. It empowers us to understand the reason why individuals act how they do, how they approach undertakings, and what propels them. We can improve our emotional intelligence and empathy by recognizing personality traits.

There are a few perceived systems and models intended to recognize and group character qualities. One of the most noticeable and generally utilized structures is the Large Five or Five Element Model (FFM), which arranges character attributes into five expansive aspects: extraversion, suitability, transparency, scruples, and neuroticism.

1. **Extraversion:** This quality alludes to a singular's degree of amiability, decisiveness, and solace in group environments. While introverts are more reserved, prefer solitude, and require time alone to recharge, extroverts are typically outgoing, energetic, and enjoy the company of others.

2. **Agreeableness**: This characteristic mirrors an individual's propensity to be helpful, humane, and thoughtful towards others. Those with a high agreeableness may be more competitive, skeptical, and less concerned with the needs of others, whereas those with a low agreeableness may be empathetic, trusting, and accommodating.

3. **Openness:** Receptiveness is described by a singular's capacity to embrace new encounters, thoughts, and viewpoints. People with a high level of openness are imaginative, inquisitive, and eager to discover new things. Then again, people low in transparency might be more customary, favor schedule, and display protection from change.

4. **Conscientiousness:** A person's level of organization, self-discipline, and dependability is referred to as their consciousness. High upright people are objective arranged, tenacious, and capable, while those low in this characteristic

might be more hasty, disordered, and need long-haul arranging capacities.

5. **Neuroticism:** The degree to which a person experiences negative emotions like anxiety, depression, and insecurity is measured by neuroticism. Those with high neuroticism will quite often be all the more impulsive, restless, and inclined to state-of-mind swings, while low neuroticism people are for the most part more settled, genuinely strong, and less responsive to push.

Perceiving these character qualities in oneself as well as other people requires perception, undivided attention, and certified interest. While there are various web-based tests and evaluations accessible that case to quantify character qualities, it is fundamental to recollect that these devices give just an overall sign and ought not be viewed as outright.

To perceive character attributes precisely, it is fundamental to think about the setting and know about different variables that might impact conduct, like social foundation, childhood, and valuable encounters. Also, it is vital to be aware of the smoothness of character qualities, as people can display various ways of behaving in different circumstances or over the long haul.

Perceiving character attributes can bring a few advantages. It enables personal development and improvement by assisting us in understanding our strengths and weaknesses. By understanding the attributes of others, we can convey all the more successfully, adjust to various social and expert conditions, and construct better connections.

In the work environment, perceiving character qualities can support framing successful groups, allotting reasonable jobs, and improving general efficiency. It engages chiefs to give proper criticism and backing to their workers, prompting expanded inspiration and occupation fulfillment. Perceiving character attributes additionally empowers people to proficiently explore clashes. By understanding others' points of view and inspirations, we can move toward conflicts with compassion and figure out some shared interests. It advances cooperation and cultivates an amicable climate in private as well as expert connections.

Being able to identify personality traits increases our emotional intelligence, aids in comprehension, and contributes to personal and interpersonal development. It is a deep-rooted excursion of investigation and understanding that permits us to see the value in the uniqueness and variety of people around the world.

3.3. Revealing Secret Thought Processes and Wants

The complexities of human psychology Humans are intricate beings. Behind each activity, there lies a rationale or want prowling in the shadows. At times, these intentions and wants are clear and effectively detectable, yet as a general rule, they stay covered up, disguised as profound inside the openings of our psyches. A fascinating journey that delves into the intricacies of human psychology is the process of comprehending and revealing these hidden motives and desires.

What drives us to act how we do? What drives our urges and desires? For centuries, philosophers, psychologists, and scientists have been baffled by these questions. The search for answers has resulted in the development of a variety of theories, methods, and studies aimed at elucidating the complex mental processes of humans.

One of the key speculations that reveal insight into stowed-away thought processes and wants is Sigmund Freud's psychoanalytic hypothesis. As per Freud, the human way of behaving is impacted by oblivious thought processes and wants that frequently originate from adolescent encounters and curbed recollections. He trusted that these secret cravings, like sexual senses, hostility, or the requirement for power, impact our activities in unpretentious yet significant ways.

Freud's hypothesis accentuated the meaning of dreams, free affiliation, and examination of mistakes, normally alluded to as Unintentional errors, as instruments to uncover these secret intentions. His progressive methodology prepared for therapy, a restorative strategy that plans to carry the oblivious intentions and wants to the cognizant level, permitting people to acquire a superior comprehension of themselves and their ways of behaving.

Clinicians and specialists keep on expanding upon Freud's hypotheses, utilizing new philosophies and procedures to uncover stowed-away thought processes and wants. One such technique is neuroimaging, which permits researchers to notice mind movement and distinguish designs related to explicit feelings and wants. By examining mind outputs and concentrating on brain connections, scientists have had the option to interface certain ways of behaving and activities to firmly established thought processes or wants that may not be evident on a superficial level.

Another methodology is social investigation, which centers

around noticing and deciphering non-verbal signs and personal conduct standards. A person's true intentions and desires can often be deduced from their facial expressions, body language, and eye movements. These unpretentious prompts, frequently compulsory and difficult to control, can double-cross secret feelings, wants, or even misleading.

The field of developmental brain research likewise disentangles stowed away thought processes and wants by looking at our way of behaving according to a transformative viewpoint. It sets that our thought processes and wants frequently originate from versatile instruments created more than millennia of human advancement. By understanding our developmental past, we can acquire knowledge of why certain thought processes and wants endure, even in present-day culture.

Understanding hidden motives and desires not only helps us gain a deeper understanding of ourselves but also of others. It permits us to have a more sympathetic and merciful way of dealing with human collaborations, as we perceive that there is something else to somebody's way of behaving besides what might be immediately obvious.

Besides, revealing secret thought processes and wants can have common applications in different fields. In business and marketing, knowing what customers want and why they want them is important for making products that meet those hidden needs and advertising campaigns that work. In treatment and advising, revealing these secret thought processes can work with recuperating and self-awareness, permitting people to manage unsettled injuries or clashes.

In any case, the excursion of revealing secret thought processes and wants isn't without its difficulties. The human brain is perplexing, and our thought processes and wants are in many cases a tangled trap of cognizant and oblivious components. Mindfulness and contemplation play a vital part in this excursion, as people should investigate their selves without predispositions or assumptions.

Additionally, covered-up thought processes and wants can be profoundly private and defenseless, making it challenging for people to share or defy them transparently. This exploration may be hindered by barriers such as the fear of being judged, rejected, or even of truly understanding oneself. Gifted specialists, therapists, or mentors can give a protected and steady climate for people to explore this multifaceted way of self-revelation.

uncovering stowed-away thought processes and wants is an entrancing excursion into the domain of human brain research. From Freud's psychoanalytic speculations to present-day neuroscience and transformative brain research, how we might interpret stowed-away inspirations has developed fundamentally. By diving into the complexities of our personalities and utilizing different methods and hypotheses, we can unwind the secrets behind our activities and gain a more profound comprehension of ourselves as well as other people. This investigation holds huge potential for self-awareness, further developed connections, and a more profound enthusiasm for the intricacies of the human experience.

CHAPTER 4

IMPACT AND NFLUENCE STRATEGY

4.1. Language and communication that is persuasive

Language and communication that is persuasive are potent instruments that have the capacity to influence or change the beliefs, attitudes, or behaviors of another person. A craftsmanship has been utilized by lawmakers, advertisers, promoters, instructors, and, surprisingly, regular people who need to persuade others regarding their perspectives or thoughts. At its center, influential language plans to convince others by engaging their feelings, thinking, or values. It includes the utilization of logical gadgets, like ethos, feeling, and logos, to convey and persuade the main interest group successfully.

Ethos relates to the believability or moral allure of the speaker or author. It includes setting up a good foundation for oneself as reliable, learned, and trustworthy. This can be accomplished through introducing proof, giving well-qualified conclusions, or exhibiting skill in the topic. For instance, a doctor who recommends a specific medication may employ ethos by highlighting their credentials and expertise in the field.

Poignancy, then again, requests to the feelings and sensations of the crowd. To pique the interest of readers or listeners, it entails employing vivid and potent language, narratives, or personal anecdotes. Commercials frequently use poignancy to bring out compassion, compassion, or energy, planning to make a profound association with the crowd and move activity. For instance, an advertisement for a charity that features a starving child evokes empathy and motivates viewers to donate.

Logos, the enticement for rationale and reason, is the third mainstay of powerful language. In order to persuade the audience, you must present solid evidence, logical reasoning, and factual information. This might incorporate insights, logical examinations, well-qualified conclusions, or coherent contentions. Legal advisors, for instance, use logos in court contentions by introducing important proof and consistent thinking to convince the jury.

Notwithstanding these logical gadgets, powerful enticing language and correspondence additionally consider the interest group's qualities, convictions, and interests. The writer or speaker can tailor their message to resonate with the audience's preexisting interests or beliefs by understanding their perspective. This can be accomplished by utilizing significant models, outlining the contention in a way that lines up with the upsides of the crowd, and tending to any potential counterarguments that might emerge.

Moreover, influential language and correspondence ought to likewise consider the medium through which the message is passed on. The selection of words, tone, and conveyance can extraordinarily affect the viability of the influential correspondence. For example, a convincing discourse conveyed in an enthusiastic and sure way can rouse and persuade the crowd in excess of a droning and unsatisfying conveyance. Notwithstanding, it is vital to take note of that while convincing language can be a useful asset, it ought to be utilized morally and dependably. Manipulative or misleading procedures ought to be stayed away from, as they sabotage the validity and reliability of the communicator. Trustworthiness and straightforwardness are key in building and keeping a veritable association with the crowd.

Powerful language and correspondence are fundamental abilities that can be used to actually impact others. One can skillfully persuade others to adopt their ideas, beliefs, or behaviors by employing rhetorical devices like ethos, pathos, and logos, comprehending the intended audience, and considering the appropriate delivery. Be that as it may, it is essential to utilize these methods morally and capably to keep up with veritable correspondence and trust between the communicator and the crowd.

4.2. Building Affinity and Laying out Trust

Building affinity and laying out trust are fundamental abilities in private and expert connections. They structure the establishment for solid associations and powerful correspondence. Whether you are a pioneer, sales rep, specialist, or essentially attempting to construct significant connections, having the option to fabricate compatibility and lay out entrust with others is central.

Compatibility can be characterized as an agreeable relationship portrayed by shared grasping, sympathy, and trust. It includes associating with people on a profound level, permitting them to feel good and comprehended. Communication becomes effortless and barriers are broken down when rapport is established.

Trust, then again, is the conviction or certainty that somebody can be depended upon or tells the truth, genuine, and skilled. It is worked over the long run through steady activities, open correspondence, and satisfying commitments. Trust is delicate and can be effectively broken, however once settled, it frames the premise areas of strength for of.

All in all, how might one form compatibility and lay out trust? Here are a few techniques:

1. **Undivided attention:** By giving them your full attention,

you can truly listen to them. This implies keeping in touch, gesturing, and answering their words. At the point when individuals feel stood by listening to, they feel esteemed and comprehended, which helps fabricate compatibility.

2. **Compassion and Understanding:** Show veritable compassion and understanding towards others' sentiments and encounters. Come at the situation from their perspective and approve their feelings. Individuals are bound to believe somebody who shows sympathy and understanding.

3. **Non-verbal correspondence:** Focus on your non-verbal communication. Keeping an open posture, emulating the other person's body language, and exuding a friendly smile can all contribute to the creation of a positive and inviting environment.

4. **Authenticity:** Be real and genuine in your cooperations. When someone is being dishonest or fake, people can tell, and trust can quickly be lost. Being sincere helps build rapport and foster trust.

5. **Consistency:** Be steady as would be natural for you and activities. Trust gradually grows when you consistently keep your promises and commitments. Then again, conflicting way of behaving can prompt uncertainty and doubt.

6. **Transparency:** Be open and straightforward in your correspondence. Share applicable data and be powerless when suitable. This straightforwardness

encourages trust and establishes a climate where individuals have a real sense of security to do likewise.

7. **Regard and Backing:** Approach others with deference, regardless of their situation or foundation. Support their thoughts, assessments, and objectives. Building compatibility and trust requires a common regard and emotionally supportive network.

8. **Confidentiality**: In the event that somebody trusts in you or offers delicate data, honor their trust by keeping up with secrecy. Honest regarding limits and taking care of special data are urgent for building trust.

9. **Follow-up and See everything through to completion**: Stay faithful to your obligations and responsibilities. Assuming you say you will follow through with something, ensure that you see everything through to completion. Over time, trust is built on this dependability.

10. **Refereeing**: Constructively resolve disagreements and conflicts. Stand by listening to alternate points of view, empower open exchange, and look for goals that are fair and advantageous together. Managing conflicts effectively contributes to strengthening relationships and fostering trust.

Establishing trust and rapport are ongoing processes that call for conscious attention, effort, and time. It is critical to recall that trust is delicate and can be effectively broken. As a result, it is absolutely necessary to cultivate and preserve these relationships by consistently exhibiting empathy, sincerity, and respect.

Building affinity and laying out trust are fundamental abilities in both individual and expert connections. People can connect with others on a deeper level through consistent actions, active listening, empathy, authenticity, and listening. Trust is worked through straightforwardness, regard, and satisfying responsibilities. These abilities can be acquired and created with work on, prompting more grounded, more significant associations.

4. 3. Overcoming Manipulation and Resistance

In today's complex and interconnected world, it is common for us to encounter manipulation and resistance in various aspects of our lives. Whether it is working, in private connections, or even inside ourselves, these powers can impede our development, achievement, and general prosperity. Nonetheless, with mindfulness, assurance, and viable techniques, it is feasible to beat obstruction and control and lead a more enabled and satisfying life.

A natural and instinctual response to change or unfamiliar circumstances is resistance. It can appear as dread, uncertainty, delaying, or whatever other way of behaving that keeps us from making a move or embracing new open doors. Resistance can be deeply rooted in our beliefs, past experiences, or fears of failure or rejection. It frequently originates from our unconscious mind.

One of the best ways of beating obstruction is through mindfulness. By looking at our viewpoints, feelings, and ways of behaving, we can distinguish the underlying drivers of our opposition and foster procedures to conquer them. This might include journaling, thoughtfulness, treatment, or other self-reflection rehearses. Understanding the hidden convictions and feelings driving our obstruction permits us to challenge them with really enabling and steady ones.

One more significant part of beating opposition is fostering a development mentality. The conviction that we can learn, develop, and adjust in any circumstance empowers us to embrace change and view it as a chance for individual and expert turn of events. By adopting a growth mindset, we can focus on the benefits and opportunities that come from overcoming resistance rather than the risks and difficulties that may arise.

Moreover, building flexibility is fundamental for beating obstruction. Strength permits us to return quickly from difficulties, difficulties, and disappointments. It includes keeping an inspirational perspective, rehearsing taking care of oneself, looking for help from others, and ceaselessly gaining from our encounters. By embracing flexibility as a lifestyle, we become more prepared to deal with and beat the opposition that might emerge.

Control, then again, includes the purposeful and frequently tricky endeavors to impact or control others. It can happen in different structures, for example, gaslighting, close-to-home control, or compulsion. Control looks to subvert our independence, certainty, and critical thinking skills. Personal boundaries are essential for standing up to manipulation. Clear limits characterize our cutoff points, values, and assumptions, and they figure out what is satisfactory and unsatisfactory in our cooperation with others. By declaring and keeping up with our limits, we can safeguard ourselves from control and pursue informed choices in light of our longings and requirements.

Furthermore, building confidence abilities is vital to defeating control. Self-assuredness includes offering our viewpoints, sentiments, and requirements in an immediate, deferential, and sure way. It permits us to convey successfully and support ourselves without depending on a forceful or inactive way of behaving. We can assert our values and priorities and resist manipulation from others by practicing assertiveness.

Developing the capacity to understand individuals at their core is one more amazing asset for defeating control. The capacity to appreciate people on a profound level includes the capacity to recognize, comprehend, and deal with our feelings as well as the feelings of others. By creating sympathy, close-to-home mindfulness, and powerful relational abilities, we can explore manipulative strategies with lucidity and trustworthiness. The ability to appreciate anyone at their core additionally empowers us to lay out credible associations and assemble better connections given trust and regard.

To successfully overcome manipulation, it is essential to cultivate a sense of self-worth and self-confidence. At the point when we trust in our worth and abilities, we are less inclined to be influenced or constrained by manipulative strategies. Building fearlessness includes perceiving our assets, commending our accomplishments, and developing a positive mental self-view. By sustaining our self-esteem, we can move toward connections and circumstances from a position of self-assuredness and oppose control.

Beating opposition and control requires a mix of mindfulness, versatility, self-assuredness, the capacity to understand individuals at their core, and certainty. By understanding the underlying drivers of opposition, taking on a development outlook, and building individual limits, we can explore through obstruction and embrace change. Similarly, by creating confidence abilities, the capacity to appreciate individuals on a profound level and self-esteem, we can safeguard ourselves from control and keep up with solid connections. It is through these endeavors that we can defeat opposition and control, and carry on with a more enabled, real, and satisfying life.

45

CHAPTER 5

GUESSING THOUGHTS IN REGULAR CIRCUMSTANCES

5 .1 Telepathy in friendly communications

Mind perusing in friendly collaborations alludes to the capacity to see and figure out somebody's viewpoints, sentiments, and expectations without direct correspondence. A fundamental ability empowers people to explore social circumstances successfully, identify with others, and layout significant associations.

While participating in friendly connections, nonverbal signals assume a huge part in passing on data past expressed words. Body language, facial expressions, voice tone, and gestures are all examples of these cues. Gifted telepaths have an increased aversion to these prompts, permitting them to interpret basic feelings and contemplations that may not be expressly expressed.

One part of telepathy includes precisely deciphering an individual's feelings. By focusing on unpretentious looks and non-verbal communication, one can acquire knowledge of how an individual genuinely feels. For instance, a slight descending look might demonstrate misery, while an open stance and loosened-up muscles might recommend satisfaction or solace. Mind readers are skilled at recognizing these cues and responding appropriately, increasing their sensitivity and empathy.

Besides, mind perusing in friendly collaborations is firmly connected with instinct. Instinct is the oblivious and programmed handling of data, which gives speedy experiences in a given circumstance or person. Mind-reading abilities can be significantly improved by combining intuition with the capacity to recognize nonverbal cues. Instinctive people have an uncanny capacity to precisely think about the thing somebody is thinking or feeling, even without unequivocal information or proof.

In addition, effective mind reading in social interactions is aided by comprehending social context and cultural norms. Various societies have differing correspondence styles, standards, and assumptions. Individuals can accurately interpret the behavior of others and respond appropriately when they are attuned to these cultural nuances. For example, in certain societies, direct eye-to-eye connection should be visible as an indication of disregard, while in others, it is an indication of mindfulness. Telepaths who comprehend these social distinctions can change their assumptions and understandings of needs, making social communications smoother and more productive.

In any case, it is critical to take note that clairvoyance is certainly not a godlike power, but rather an expertise that can be created through training and experience. It requires a functioning perception of verbal and nonverbal prompts, as well as a capacity to imagine someone else's perspective. Individuals can increase their social intelligence and build stronger relationships with others by perfecting their mind-reading skills.

It is essential to emphasize that mind reading should be used ethically and compassionately. It is essential to keep in mind that, even though it can provide valuable insights, it is not a tool for controlling someone's emotions or invading their privacy. It ought to be utilized to more readily grasp others, offer help, and assemble positive connections. Mind perusing in friendly connections is an important expertise that includes seeing and grasping somebody's considerations, sentiments, and goals through nonverbal prompts and instinct. It assists people with exploring social circumstances, laying out sympathy, and fabricating significant associations. By effectively noticing and deciphering the signs and signals given by others, it is feasible to upgrade one's clairvoyance powers and work on friendly insight.

5.2 Telepathy in business and dealings

Mind perusing in business and talks is an idea that has acquired critical consideration as of late. As innovation keeps on propelling, specialists and organizations the same are investigating ways of understanding and foresee the attitude of their partners to have an advantage in talks and eventually go with better business choices.

The capacity to guess thoughts might seem like something out of a sci-fi novel, however, it has turned into a reality as different mental procedures and innovations. Organizations have understood that effective dealings depend on the benefits of their proposition as well as on figuring out the necessities, inspirations, and manners of thinking of the other party.

One part of telepathy in business and talks is the utilization of non-verbal communication and non-verbal prompts. Specialists in the field of discussion brain research have recognized explicit motions, looks, and stances that can uncover stowed-away considerations and expectations. Via cautiously noticing these non-verbal prompts, moderators can acquire important bits of knowledge into the mentality of their partners and change their methodology likewise.

Notwithstanding non-verbal communication, the investigation of microexpressions and facial acknowledgment innovation has shown promising outcomes in unraveling feelings and contemplations during exchanges. Microexpressions are compulsory looks that uncover temporary feelings, and they can give significant insights into somebody's actual sentiments and expectations. Facial acknowledgment programming can dissect these microexpressions progressively, permitting mediators to measure the viability of their recommendations and make essential changes.

One more type of telepathy in business talks is the utilization of social financial aspects, which joins experiences from brain research and financial aspects to comprehend the reason why individuals settle on specific choices. By understanding the basic mental predispositions that influence direction, arbitrators can expect and address likely complaints or counterarguments ahead of time. This information permits them to approach their recommendations in a manner that lines up with the mental predispositions of the other party and improves the probability of an effective exchange.

Progressions in innovation have additionally extended the potential outcomes of telepathy in business and exchanges. For instance, neuroimaging strategies, for example, useful attractive reverberation imaging (fMRI) can give continuous data about cerebrum movement during exchanges. By breaking down the brain correspondence of independent direction, specialists can acquire a more profound comprehension of how people process data and simply decide. This information can be utilized to tailor exchange procedures and increment the possibilities of a great result.

Moreover, AI calculations and man-made brainpower can examine huge datasets and recognize designs that people might ignore. By investigating past dealings, these calculations can foresee the logical results of future exchanges in light of different boundaries, for example, the discussion style of the other party, the business, and, surprisingly, the hour of the day. This prescient capacity enables arbitrators to go with additional educated choices and increment their possibilities regarding achievement. While mind perusing in business and dealings presents energizing open doors, there are moral contemplations that should be tended to. The intrusion of protection and the potential for control are worries that should be viewed seriously. It is pivotal to guarantee that the utilization of clairvoyance procedures and innovations is done straightforwardly, with educated assent regarding all gatherings included.

Mind perusing in business and discussions is a captivating field that holds extraordinary potential for further developing direction and accomplishing fruitful results. By utilizing experiences from brain research, non-verbal communication examination, social financial matters, and trend-setting innovations, arbitrators can acquire important information about the contemplations, feelings, and inspirations of their partners. Notwithstanding, moral contemplations should continuously be at the bleeding edge, and the utilization of clairvoyance procedures ought to be done dependably and with full consciousness of its suggestions.

5.3. Mind perusing in private connections

Mind perusing in private relationships is a perplexing and captivating point. It alludes to the capacity to comprehend and understand the considerations, sentiments, and expectations of our accomplices without them unequivocally communicating them.

In connections, we frequently take a stab at a profound association and understanding with our soul mate. Mind perusing can be viewed as an easy route to accomplishing this degree of closeness and closeness. It includes focusing on non-verbal prompts, non-verbal communication, and feelings to unravel what our accomplice is thinking or feeling.

While mind perusing can improve correspondence and profound association, it additionally accompanies its reasonable portion of difficulties. One of the primary difficulties is the potential for distortion. We might think we can read our accomplice's mind, however actually, our presumptions can be not even close to precise. This can prompt false impressions, struggle, and, surprisingly, broken trust.

Additionally, mind perusing can likewise prompt unreasonable assumptions. We might begin anticipating that our accomplices should expect our necessities and wants without us imparting them unequivocally. This can put an extra weight on our connections as they battle to satisfy our unexpressed assumptions.

One more downside of clairvoyance is the expected attack on security. At the point when we attempt to guess what our accomplice might be thinking, we may accidentally attack their own profound space. Everybody merits security, and continually attempting to dive into their viewpoints can be meddlesome and harmful to the relationship.

Then again, while mind perusing is drawn closer with wariness and responsiveness, it tends to be a useful asset for creating the capacity to understand individuals on a deeper level and compassion. It can assist us with turning out to be more receptive to our accomplice's necessities and can prompt further close-to-home association. When utilized fittingly, mind perusing can improve correspondence, resolve clashes, and make a more amicable relationship.

The following are a couple of techniques to consolidate sound mind reading in private connections:

1. **Undivided attention:** Focus on your accomplice's words, tone, and non-verbal communication. Be completely present during discussions and attempt to grasp their hidden feelings and goals.

2. **Compassion**: Come at the situation from your accomplice's perspective and attempt to grasp their viewpoint. This can assist you with expecting their responses and feelings all the more precisely.

3. **Open Correspondence**: Clairvoyance ought to never supplant open correspondence. Urge your accomplice to unequivocally offer their viewpoints and sentiments. Make a place of refuge where they feel open to imparting their deepest contemplations to you.

4. **Shared Understanding**: Telepathy works best when the two accomplices are effectively participating in seeing each other's feelings and necessities. Support a culture of receptiveness and understanding where the two accomplices can openly communicate their thoughts.

5. **Registration:** Rather than accepting, inquire as to whether you are

accurately figuring out their viewpoints or feelings. This can forestall errors and assist with building trust.

Keep in mind, that mind perusing is not an enchanted power, and it's anything but a substitute for direct correspondence. While it can extend close to the home association and advance comprehension, it ought to constantly be drawn nearer with deference, awareness, and the affirmation that suspicions may in some cases be mistaken. By consolidating mind perusing with open correspondence, trust, and compassion, we can make better and more satisfying individual connections.

JUDY THEODORAH

CHAPTER 6

MORAL CONTEMPLATIONS

6.1 Regarding limits and security

Regarding limits and security are pivotal parts of building sound and positive connections, both individual and expert. It includes recognizing and regarding someone else's very own space, feelings, choices, and data. Regarding limits and protection shows sympathy, understanding, and empathy yet in addition cultivates trust, common regard, and correspondence inside connections.

Limits allude as far as possible and rules that people set for themselves to safeguard their physical, close to home, and mental prosperity. These limits can change from one individual to another, contingent upon their qualities, convictions, and individual encounters. Regarding these limits implies understanding and tolerating somebody's very own cutoff points without forcing or encroaching upon them.

Protection, then again, relates to a singular's more right than wrong to keep specific parts of their life secret. This can incorporate individual data, considerations, sentiments, and encounters that they probably shouldn't impart to other people. Regarding protection includes perceiving and recognizing these limits, ceasing from meddlesome or attacking somebody's very own space, and regarding their requirement for privacy and independence.

One of the crucial motivations behind why we ought to regard limits and protection is to lay out and keep up with sound connections. By perceiving and regarding somebody's limits, we show them that we worth and regard their independence and distinction. This can establish a protected and agreeable climate for open correspondence and trust to prosper. At the point when individuals feel that their limits and security are regarded, they are bound to feel appreciated, comprehended, and acknowledged inside their connections.

Regarding limits and security likewise forestalls false impressions and clashes. At the point when we dismissal or disregard somebody's limits, we risk violating our limits and interrupting their own space. This can prompt distress, pressure, and even hatred inside connections. By being aware of the cutoff points set by others, we can develop better and more amicable communications.

One more essential part of regarding limits and protection is perceiving and tolerating that every individual has various requirements and inclinations. What may be adequate to one individual may not be to another. By turning out to be more mindful of these distinctions, we can adjust our ways of behaving and activities as needs be. This ability to adjust not just exhibits our sympathy and regard for other people yet additionally advances inclusivity and enthusiasm for different viewpoints and encounters.

In a computerized age where innovation empowers practically prompt correspondence, regarding limits and privacy is considerably more essential. It is fundamental to recollect that individuals reserve the option to figure out what they share and with whom they share it. Whether it is private data, sentiments, or pictures, we should constantly look for assent prior to sharing whatever might attack somebody's security.

Regarding limits and security is similarly critical in proficient settings. Businesses and partners ought to effectively encourage a climate where people feel open to communicating their cutoff points and concerns. This incorporates regarding individual space, abstaining from meddling or spreading individual data, and guaranteeing that delicate information stays secure and classified.

Regarding limits and protection is essential to solid connections, trust, and compelling correspondence. By recognizing and regarding somebody's very own cutoff points and classification, we show compassion, understanding, and regard. Besides, it encourages a climate where people are open to communicating their thoughts, prompting more noteworthy by and large prosperity and agreement in all parts of life. Thus, we should all put forth a cognizant attempt to regard limits and security, both disconnected and on the web, and make an existence where everybody has a solid sense of reassurance and esteemed.

6.2: Utilizing mind perusing Dependably

In reality as we know it where innovation keeps on progressing at an unprecedented speed, the idea of telepathy could appear as though something straight out of a sci-fi film. Notwithstanding, late progressions in neuroscience have carried us nearer to understanding and possibly outfitting the force of our brains. While mind perusing can possibly reform different fields, it is critical to capably perceive the moral ramifications and utilize this power.

Mind perusing innovation includes the utilization of strategies, for example, utilitarian attractive reverberation imaging (fMRI) and electroencephalography (EEG) to distinguish and decipher cerebrum action. This innovation might possibly give bits of knowledge into a singular's viewpoints, feelings, and expectations, which could have huge ramifications in different fields, including medical services, schooling, advertising, and policing.

In the field of medical care, mind perusing can offer significant experiences into psychological wellness conditions like gloom, nervousness, and schizophrenia. This innovation can assist medical care experts with identifying early advance notice signs and give customized therapy plans to patients. By understanding the basic instruments of psychological maladjustments, mind perusing innovation can open up new roads for different treatment choices and worked on tolerant consideration.

In training, mind perusing can reform the manner in which we learn and educate. By examining cerebrum action, teachers can fit informative materials and procedures to individual understudies, improving their opportunity for growth. This can assist with tending to the different requirements of understudies, making training more comprehensive and powerful.

Mind perusing likewise can possibly change the universe of showcasing. By understanding buyers' mind reactions to commercials or items, advertisers can make more designated and engaging efforts. This can bring about expanded deals and consumer loyalty. In any case, it is vital to guarantee that people's security is safeguarded in this specific situation. Severe rules and guidelines ought to be set up to guarantee that individual considerations and feelings are not taken advantage of or controlled for business gain.

In policing, perusing innovation might possibly support criminal examinations. It can assist with distinguishing likely suspects, decide the veracity of declarations, and even forestall violations before they happen. Notwithstanding, the utilization of clairvoyance in policing huge worries about security, individual freedoms, and the potential for misuse. Severe guidelines and oversight are important to guarantee that this innovation is utilized dependably and inside the limits of the law.

While the likely advantages of telepathy innovation are tremendous, accentuating the dependable utilization of this possibly nosy power is significant. The moral ramifications of clairvoyance innovation can't be put into words. Individual protection and assent ought to be at the very front of any contemplations including mind perusing.

Informed assent, most importantly, is principal. People ought to be completely mindful of the innovation being utilized, the reason for its application, and the potential dangers implied. Assent ought to be gotten in a straightforward and far reaching way, guaranteeing that people have a certified decision in partaking or quitting.

Security insurance ought to likewise be a first concern. People's own considerations and feelings ought to be treated with the highest level of awareness and privacy. Information gathered through mind perusing innovation ought to be safely put away and simply available to approved staff. Severe guidelines ought to be set up to forestall any abuse or unapproved admittance to this information.

Moreover, shields should be set up to address possible predispositions and to guarantee fair and impartial treatment of people. Understanding of telepathy information ought to be finished via prepared experts, directed by laid out moral rules. Calculations utilized in information examination ought to be consistently evaluated and tried to limit the gamble of predisposition or oppressive practices.

Moreover, given the potential for mind perusing innovation to be abused or taken advantage of, there should be extensive legitimate systems and guidelines set up. These structures ought to oversee the utilization and sending of telepathy innovation, framing the obligations and constraints of different partners included.

Eventually, the dependable utilization of clairvoyance innovation requires an aggregate exertion from researchers, policymakers, and society all in all. Moral conversations and discussions encompassing this innovation ought to be energized, and guidelines ought to be constantly refreshed to stay up with headways and address arising moral difficulties.

Utilizing mind perusing capably isn't just about moderating likely dangers and concerns; it is tied in with guaranteeing that this innovation upgrades our lives while maintaining major common liberties and values. By embracing a dependable methodology, we can saddle the force of clairvoyance to open its maximum capacity and have significant constructive outcome across different spaces of human life.

6.3. Self-awareness and strengthening

Self-awareness and improvement are fundamental

parts of a satisfying and fruitful life. They include constantly working on oneself, extending one's abilities and capacities, and acquiring certainty to conquer difficulties. Guaranteeing self-improvement and strengthening requires a mix of mindfulness, assurance, and a proactive way to deal with learning and advancement. This article will investigate different systems and methods to encourage self-improvement and engage people to arrive at their maximum capacity.

Mindfulness, most importantly, is the establishment for self-awareness and strengthening. It includes figuring out one's assets, shortcomings, values, and interests. Mindfulness empowers people to distinguish regions for development and foster an unmistakable vision of their own and proficient objectives. It likewise helps in perceiving and conquering self-restricting convictions and embracing a development outlook. Rehearsing self-reflection, looking for criticism from others, and taking part in exercises, for example, journaling or contemplation can upgrade mindfulness and set up for self-awareness.

Defining clear and feasible objectives is one more significant part of self-awareness and strengthening. By characterizing explicit and quantifiable targets, people can concentrate their endeavors and keep tabs on their development over the long haul. Objectives can be present moment or long haul and can connect with different everyday issues, including vocation, connections, wellbeing, or self-awareness. Separating bigger objectives into more modest, noteworthy advances can make them more reasonable and increment inspiration. Routinely checking on and changing objectives as conditions change is likewise vital to guarantee proceeded with self-improvement.

Persistent learning and improvement assume a crucial part in self-awareness and strengthening. Effectively looking for new information and abilities encourages scholarly development and extends one's capacities. This can be accomplished through different means, for example, going to studios or preparing programs, understanding books or articles, paying attention to digital recordings or book recordings, or taking web-based courses. Participating in testing errands or ventures and looking for assorted viewpoints additionally animates self-improvement. Embracing a development outlook, which puts stock in the capacity to create and work on through exertion and devotion, is fundamental for seeking after long lasting learning and accomplishing self-awareness.

Self-improvement and strengthening are not single undertakings; they additionally flourish in a climate that offers help and consolation. Building areas of strength for an organization of companions, coaches, or partners who share comparable qualities and yearnings can give inspiration, direction, and responsibility. Participating in discussions and joint efforts with others can offer new points of view and new learning valuable open doors. Looking for useful input from believed people can likewise assist with recognizing vulnerable sides and regions for development. Furthermore, encircling oneself with positive and rousing impacts, whether through books, digital broadcasts, or positive connections, can add to self-improvement and strengthening.

Dealing with one's physical and mental prosperity is basic for self-awareness and strengthening. Focusing on taking care of oneself exercises, like activity, legitimate nourishment, and rest, upholds by and large wellbeing and increments energy levels. Participating in exercises that give pleasure and unwinding, like leisure activities, contemplation, or investing energy in nature, lessens pressure and improves close to home prosperity. Emotional well-being is similarly significant; looking for proficient assistance or directing when required can give important experiences and instruments to self-awareness.

Removing chances and venturing from one's usual range of familiarity is fundamental for self-improvement and strengthening. Embracing difficulties and survey disappointments as learning open doors cultivates versatility and self-improvement. Attempting new exercises, taking on influential positions, or seeking after new ways permits people to find their secret potential and fabricate certainty. Defeating fears and confronting deterrents head-on prompts self-awareness and strengthening.

Guaranteeing self-improvement and strengthening requires a proactive and deliberate way to deal with one's own turn of events. It involves mindfulness, laying out clear objectives, consistent learning, and looking for help. Self-improvement and strengthening are not straight cycles yet rather deep rooted ventures. By embracing self-reflection, learning, and taking care of oneself, people can open their maximum capacity and carry on with a satisfying and enabled life.

65

CHAPTER 7

ADVANCE METHODS

7.1 Mentalism and the Specialty of Deception: Revealing the Insider facts of the Psyche

Mentalism is an intriguing type of diversion that includes performing and making deceptions that give the presence of telepathy, expectation, and other phenomenal mental capacities. A performing craftsmanship has spellbound crowds for a really long time, leaving them in stunningness and miracle. Mentalists consolidate sorcery stunts, brain science, and dramatic skill to make an encounter that challenges clarification. In this article, we will investigate the captivating universe of mentalism and dive into the mysteries behind the specialty of deception.

Starting points of Mentalism:

To comprehend the specialty of mentalism, it is fundamental to dive into its authentic beginnings. The expression "mentalism" was first authored by French performer Jules de Jonnes in the last part of the 1800s. Notwithstanding, the underlying foundations of this work of art date back a lot further. Mentalism can be followed back to old times when shamans, prophets, and prophets were accepted to have extraordinary capacities to speak with spirits and anticipate what's to come.

In the advanced period, mentalism acquired prevalence in the late nineteenth and mid twentieth hundreds of years with pioneers like Alexander Herrmann, Joseph Dunninger, and Harry Houdini. These famous figures performed mind-perusing acts that staggered crowds in vaudeville theaters, causing a buzz and making ready for contemporary mentalists.

The Methods:

Mentalism depends on a mix of mental standards, skillful deception, confusion, and ability to entertain to make the deception of telepathy. Mentalists frequently utilize different procedures to achieve apparently incomprehensible accomplishments. We should investigate the absolute most usually utilized ones:

1. **Cold Perusing:** Cold perusing is an expertise that permits mentalists to give people precise and explicit data about their own lives with practically no earlier information. This procedure includes cautiously noticing the subject's non-verbal communication, verbal prompts, and outward presentation to make ballpark estimations about their experience, character, and interests.

2. **Hot Perusing**: Hot perusing is a method that includes getting data about a person before the presentation

covertly. This should be possible by having an associate assemble data or using different internet based sources like web-based entertainment profiles. Equipped with this data, the mentalist can give the presence of having powerful information, leaving the crowd surprised.

3. **Mental Control**: Mentalists are specialists in taking advantage of mental predispositions and mental standards to make the deception of psyche control. They utilize inconspicuous idea, confusion, and driving inquiries to significantly mold the considerations and choices of their subjects, causing it to seem like they can understand minds or foresee what's in store.

4. **Skillful deception**: Mentalists additionally utilize skillful deception methods ordinarily connected with customary sorcery to improve their exhibitions. They could utilize different props, like playing a game of cards, envelopes, or different items, to make deceptions that resist clarification.

Morals and Amusement:

Mentalism obscures the line among deception and reality, provoking conversations about morals and the potential mischief it can cause. Some contend that mentalism can control weak people or propagate deceptions in heavenly capacities. Nonetheless, mentalists frequently accentuate that their exhibitions are only for diversion purposes. They endeavor to make an enamoring experience that permits individuals to suspend their mistrust and experience wonder. It is essential for mentalists to keep up with straightforwardness and not exploit or trick their crowd.

Mentalism is a many-sided fine art that joins brain research, dramatic skill, and deception to make stunning exhibitions. It has advanced over hundreds of years and keeps on enthralling crowds around the world. Whether it's anticipating the future, mind-perusing, or bowing spoons, mentalism challenges our impression of the real world and leaves us doubting the constraints of human potential. While the mysteries behind mentalism might lie in mental strategies, confusion, and skillful deception, the genuine wizardry of mentalism lies in the capacity to suspend skepticism and make an extraordinary encounter. It is a demonstration of the force of the human brain and our natural longing to put stock in the uncommon. So next time you witness a mentalist in real life, permit yourself to be flabbergasted and let the marvels of the brain unwind before your eyes.

7.2 Dominating cold perusing: The Specialty of Influence and Understanding

Cold perusing is a work of art that has captivated the two entertainers and crowds for quite a long time. It is the ability of compellingly perusing somebody's character, qualities, and history with no earlier information or data. This capacity to dig into the profundities of someone else's mind and uncover perspectives concealed to the unaided eye is frequently utilized by mentalists, mystics, and entertainers to make a remarkable encounter for their crowd. Be that as it may, cold perusing isn't restricted to diversion purposes alone; it has reasonable applications in different fields like brain research, deals, exchange, and, surprisingly, regular connections.

The most important move towards dominating virus perusing is fostering major areas of strength for an of perception. You can pick up on subtle cues, body language, and nonverbal communication that can give you valuable insight into a person's thoughts and feelings if you are observant. Focus on microexpressions, changes in stance, and eye developments as they can be marks of hidden feelings or considerations.

One more fundamental part of cold perusing is the capacity to rapidly construct affinity. Laying out compatibility makes trust and a feeling of association, making the individual more helpless to open up and share data. This can be accomplished by reflecting non-verbal communication, talking at a comparative speed, and showing certifiable interest in the individual's encounters and stories.

In cold reading, active listening is a crucial skill. By effectively tuning in, you can comprehend the verbally expressed words as well as recognize examples and subtleties in their way of discourse. Notice their selection of words, tone, and mood as they can give significant bits of knowledge into their character qualities, values, and convictions. As a cool peruser, you should have areas of strength for an and imaginative reasoning skills. Fostering a collection of general proclamations that apply to many people is critical. These assertions ought to be unassuming, permitting the individual to give more data and empowering you to expand upon it. By consolidating explicit subtleties shared by the individual, you can give the deception of having a more profound understanding into their life.

The use of Barnum statements, named after the famous showman P.T. Barnum, is another cold reading technique. Barnum proclamations are general explanations that appear to be exceptionally customized yet are, as a matter of fact, pertinent to a huge level of the populace. By integrating these assertions into your virus perusing, you can give the impression of having restrictive information about the individual.

It is fundamental to keep a sympathetic and non-critical demeanor during the virus understanding interaction. Individuals are bound to open up and share data on the off chance that they feel upheld and comprehended. Try not to make snap decisions or suppositions, as it can obstruct the precision of your perusing and possibly insult the individual. Practice is the way to dominating virus perusing. Begin by rehearsing with loved ones, step by step extending your abilities to outsiders. It is crucial for note that chilly perusing ought to continuously be performed morally and with the assent of the individual in question. It ought to never be utilized to control or mischief others yet rather as a device for knowledge, understanding, and diversion.

Excelling at cold perusing requires a mix of perception, undivided attention, creative mind, and compatibility building abilities. It is a work of art that can be applied in different settings and can extraordinarily upgrade your capacity to comprehend and associate with others. Make sure to move toward cold perusing morally and mindfully, continuously regarding the limits and assent of the people in question. With training and commitment, you can turn into a genuine expert of the art, opening the secret insider facts of the human psyche.

7.3. Growing your clairvoyance capacities

Clairvoyance, the capacity to impart considerations and sentiments without the utilization of expressed words or actual signals, has for some time been a subject of interest and interest. While customarily thought to be a paranormal peculiarity, many accept that clairvoyance is an intrinsic human capacity that can be created and extended with training and expectation. Extending your clairvoyant capacities goes past the domains of sci-fi and into the domain of self-improvement and self-revelation. It opens up a totally different universe of potential outcomes and associations by improving the manner in which we speak with others and at last, ourselves.

To start extending your clairvoyant capacities, it means

a lot to begin with a groundwork of mindfulness and care. Fostering your very own sharp feeling contemplations, sentiments, and goals is significant to become receptive to the nuances of clairvoyant correspondence.

Meditation is an important practice for increasing self-awareness. Ordinary reflection assists with calming the psyche and permits you to notice your contemplations without getting snatched up by them. You can build a solid foundation for telepathic communication by gaining a deeper understanding of your own mental and emotional processes through meditation.

You can begin to investigate the idea of energetic resonance once you have developed a sense of self-awareness. Fiery reverberation is the possibility that all that in the universe is comprised of energy and vibrates at its own special recurrence. By adjusting yourself to the frequencies of others, you can more readily figure out their viewpoints and feelings, and work with clairvoyant correspondence.

To foster your capacity to impact others, developing sympathy and compassion is significant. These characteristics permit you to profoundly comprehend and associate with the encounters of others, making it simpler to tune into their lively frequencies. Carving out opportunity to effectively tune in and understand others will improve your clairvoyant capacities and reinforce your associations with everyone around you.

One more incredible asset for growing clairvoyant capacities is representation. Representation includes making mental pictures and situations to assist with refining your aims and convey them to other people. By rehearsing perception works out, you can fortify your capacity to send and get clairvoyant messages.

One famous perception procedure is to envision sending and getting light emissions to and from others. By envisioning these light emissions, you can make a strong vigorous association with others and open up stations for clairvoyant correspondence. It is essential to rehearse representations consistently to fortify your capacities and make them more available in day to day existence.

Using telepathic tools and exercises, in addition to meditation, empathy, and visualization, can help you improve your abilities. These devices can incorporate clairvoyance cards, where you endeavor to figure the image or word on a card that someone else is holding, or essentially rehearsing clairvoyant correspondence practices with an accomplice.

One fundamental clairvoyant activity includes sitting in a peaceful space with an accomplice, and intellectually sending and getting basic messages. Begin with straightforward considerations or pictures, for example, blue or the picture of an apple. Practice with your accomplice, and steadily increment the intricacy of the messages as you become more capable. Moving toward the development of clairvoyant capacities with a receptive outlook and a feeling of curiosity is significant. Comprehend that progress might be slow and that results may not be prompt or unmistakable all of the time. The personal development of telepathic abilities necessitates perseverance, self-awareness, and consistent practice.

Growing your clairvoyant capacities offers the possibility to open an unheard of degree of human association and understanding. You can tap into this innate ability and enhance your communication skills on a profound and energetic level by developing self-awareness, empathy, visualization, and telepathic tools and exercises. Embrace the test and partake in the excursion as you open the secret domains of clairvoyance inside yourself.

CHAPTER 8

DIFFICULTIES AND IMPEDIMENTS

8.1. Conquering road obstructions as a main priority in perusing

Mind perusing is the phenomenal capacity to peruse the contemplations and expectations of others, yet it is an expertise that many individuals long to have. Having the option to interface with others on a more profound level and have knowledge into their deepest contemplations is without a doubt an enticing possibility. In any case, very much like some other expertise, it accompanies its own arrangement of difficulties and road obstructions that one should survive.

One of the significant detours as a main priority perusing is the innate intricacy of the human brain itself. Our brains are a trap of contemplations, feelings, and discernments, continually changing and developing. Attempting to explore this perplexing maze can be overpowering, in any event, for the most experienced experts. It requires a profound comprehension of brain science, non-verbal communication, and human way of behaving.

Another significant barrier is the impedance of outside factors. Our considerations and expectations are affected by various outside variables like our environmental factors, current temperament, and individual predispositions. These outside variables can frequently cloud our capacity to guess what somebody might be thinking precisely. For instance, somebody might show non-verbal communication that recommends they are lying, however it very well may be because of their distress in the climate, as opposed to a conscious demonstration of trickery.

Moreover, mind perusing can be obstructed by the absence of trust and affinity between people. Building trust is vital in any relational relationship, as it establishes a climate where individuals feel happy with sharing their actual contemplations and expectations. Without trust, it turns out to be incredibly difficult to precisely guess what somebody might be thinking, as they might keep or hide data from you.

Beating these barricades requires tirelessness, persistence, and a readiness to persistently learn and develop. Here are a few methodologies that can help in defeating the detours as a primary concern perusing:

1. **Foster a profound comprehension of human way of behaving:** To precisely guess what somebody might be thinking, you should initially grasp the complexities of human way of behaving. This includes concentrating on brain research, non-verbal communication, and non-verbal prompts. By sharpening your insight here, you

can all the more likely decipher the signs that individuals unknowingly radiate.

2. **Develop undivided attention abilities:** Listening is a fundamental part of clairvoyance. Effectively paying attention to what others are talking about, as well as noticing their non-verbal communication, can give important experiences into their viewpoints and expectations. Try not to rush to make judgment calls and on second thought center around genuinely figuring out the other individual.

3. **Assemble trust and compatibility**: Building trust is significant at the top of the priority list perusing. Show veritable interest, compassion, and regard for the other individual's sentiments and suppositions. This will make an environment of trust and receptiveness, making it more straightforward for them to share their considerations and aims.

4. **Develop the capacity to appreciate anyone on a profound level:** The capacity to understand people on a deeper level is the capacity to perceive, comprehend, and deal with our own feelings, as well as the feelings of others. Creating the capacity to appreciate anyone on a profound level can fundamentally improve your telepathy powers, as it permits you to all the more likely figure out the feelings and inspirations driving individuals' considerations and ways of behaving.

5. **Practice care and mindfulness**: Care and mindfulness

are useful assets in beating barriers at the top of the priority list perusing. By rehearsing care, you can prepare your psyche to zero in on the current second and check out the considerations and ways of behaving of others. Mindfulness, then again, assists you with understanding your own inclinations and assumptions, empowering you to move toward mind perusing with an unmistakable and unprejudiced outlook.

6. **Gain as a matter of fact and criticism:** Clairvoyance is definitely not a careful science and requires ceaseless learning and improvement. Gain from your encounters and look for criticism from others. Consider your triumphs and disappointments, and use them as any open doors for development and advancement.

Conquering barricades as a main priority perusing is a difficult undertaking that requires devotion and a profound comprehension of human way of behaving. By fostering a rich information on brain research, improving undivided attention abilities, building trust and compatibility, developing capacity to understand people on a profound level, rehearsing care and mindfulness, and consistently gaining from encounters, one can explore the perplexing scene of the human psyche and upgrade their capacity to peruse the considerations and expectations of others precisely.

8.2 Tolerating the constraints of your capacities

Tolerating the constraints of your capacities is a

fundamental part of self-awareness and mindfulness. It includes perceiving and grasping your assets and shortcomings, and being practical about what you can accomplish. While it tends to be trying to recognize our constraints, doing so can prompt a really satisfying and effective life.

One of the key motivations behind why tolerating our cutoff points is significant is that it assists us with laying out sensible objectives. At the point when we know about our capacities and restrictions, we can make reachable objectives that line up with our abilities and potential. This empowers us to pursue goals that are inside our span, prompting a more prominent probability of progress and a feeling of satisfaction. Running against the norm, laying out ridiculous objectives in view of misleading suspicions about our capacities can bring about dissatisfaction and disappointment, frustrating our advancement and confidence.

Tolerating the restrictions of our capacities additionally permits us to go with better choices. At the point when we know about our assets and shortcomings, we can settle on informed decisions about the undertakings and activities we take on. It assists us with distinguishing regions where we might require support or extra assets, permitting us to pursue choices that expand our odds of coming out on top. By understanding our cutoff points, we can try not to be overpowered by liabilities that surpass our capacities, in this way forestalling burnout and stress.

Also, tolerating the constraints of our capacities helps encourage self-empathy. It is critical to recognize that no one is awesome and that everybody has their own arrangement of impediments. By tolerating our restrictions, we can treat ourselves with benevolence and understanding when confronted with difficulties or misfortunes. Rather than being excessively basic or unforgiving on ourselves, we can embrace a more caring outlook and spotlight on self-awareness instead of flawlessness.

Besides, tolerating our cutoff points permits us to really use our assets. At the point when we get it and acknowledge what we are great at, we can focus our endeavors on regions where we succeed. This empowers us to contribute our abilities and aptitude to different parts of our own and proficient lives, improving our general execution and fulfillment. By utilizing our assets, we can likewise work together with other people who have integral capacities, cultivating collaboration and making aggregate progress.

Tolerating the restrictions of our capacities is certainly not an indication of shortcoming or disappointment; it is an indication of development and mindfulness. It empowers us to take full advantage of our assets, put forth feasible objectives, and pursue informed choices. It additionally adds to our general prosperity by diminishing pressure and cultivating self-empathy. By getting it and tolerating our limits, we can explore through existence with more prominent clearness, reason, and satisfaction.

8.3. Nonstop learning and improvement

Nonstop learning and improvement is the most common way of procuring new information, abilities, and methods all through one's life to upgrade individual and expert turn of events. In today's rapidly changing world, it is a mindset that places a high value on progress and growth.

The ability to learn and adapt is more important than ever in the global economy of today, where competition is fierce. The fast speed of innovative headways and the rising intricacy of different enterprises require people to acquire and overhaul their abilities ceaselessly. What could have been viewed as adequate information and abilities a couple of years prior may as of now not be pertinent or successful today. Consistent learning permits people to remain current and important in their fields, guaranteeing their drawn-out progress and employability.

Persistent learning offers various advantages on both individual and expert levels. On an individual level, learning new things keeps our psyches sharp and dynamic. It makes us more curious and creative, broadens our horizons, and helps us understand the world around us. It upgrades our decisive reasoning and critical thinking abilities, empowering us to move toward difficulties with new thoughts and creative arrangements. Persistent advancement likewise supports our fearlessness and confidence, as we gain a feeling of achievement and self-awareness with each new expertise procured or information get a handle on.

On an expert level, constant learning is critical to consider professional success. It enables individuals to capitalize on emerging opportunities and maintain their competitive edge. By ceaselessly learning and improving, experts can extend their ability, and increment their worth in the gig market, and entryways to previously unheard-of vocation possibilities. Employers are more likely to look for continuous learners because of their resilience, adaptability, and commitment to their development.

Besides, consistent learning adds to generally speaking authoritative achievement. Organizations that develop a culture of ceaseless learning among their workers will generally be more creative, strong, and versatile to change. They are better prepared to explore through vulnerabilities and difficulties, and they are bound to quickly jump all over chances and remain cutthroat. Ceaseless learning upgrades representative commitment and fulfillment, lessening turnover rates and encouraging a positive workplace. It additionally drives innovativeness and information sharing inside groups, prompting further developed critical thinking and dynamic limits.

So, how can people embrace continuous improvement

and learning? Some effective methods include:

1. **Embrace a development outlook:** Taking on an outlook that puts stock in the potential for development and improvement is significant. Embrace difficulties, gain from disappointments, and consider misfortunes to be chances to learn and move along.

2. **Regularly practice learning:** Distribute standard time for realizing, whether it's understanding books, taking web-based courses, going to studios, or participating in conversations with specialists. Create a learning strategy and specific goals to ensure ongoing progress.

3. **Look for different learning and valuable open doors:** Investigate different wellsprings of information and encounters. Go to gatherings and workshops, join proficient organizations, and team up with assorted people to acquire alternate points of view and bits of knowledge.

4. **Be interested and clarify pressing issues**: Constantly clarify some pressing issues, look for explanations, and challenge existing presumptions. Interest drives learning and invigorates scholarly development.

5. **Embrace input:** Be willing to hear what other people have to say. Useful analysis can be an important instrument for development, featuring vulnerable sides and regions for development.

6. **Think about past experiences:** Cut out a potential chance to consider past experiences and focus on

representations learned. Which worked honorably? What could have been done differently? Reflection assists with personal development and improvement.

7. **Apply data**: Set what you have acknowledged up as an ordinary event. Apply new capacities and information, taking everything into account, conditions to develop learning and strengthen ability.

Persistent learning and improvement are fundamental in the present unique world. It upgrades self-improvement and advancement as well as adds to the outcome of associations. People can stay ahead of the curve, adapt to new challenges, and thrive in their personal and professional lives by adopting a mindset of continuous learning. In this way, let us concede to long-lasting learning and seek constantly information and improvement.

CHAPTER 9

THE TELEPATHY TOOL COMPARTMENTS

9.1 Instruments and Assets for Telepathy: Investigating the Universe of Mentalism

Mind perusing, an idea that has interested people for a long time, keeps on spellbinding our creative minds even today. Mind reading is a skill that can be developed and honed with the right tools and resources, although it may appear to be something out of a sci-fi movie or a supernatural ability. In this article, we will explore the world of mentalism as well as the various resources and tools that are available to those who are interested in mind reading.

1. **Books:** For learning about mind-reading methods and principles, books are an invaluable resource. There are a few very much regarded writers in the field of mentalism who have composed widely regarding the matter. A few prominent names incorporate Derren Brown, Banachek, and Sway Cassidy, among others. These writers give bits of knowledge into different strategies like virus perusing, mental control, and the utilization of non-verbal prompts to deduce data. Perusing books on mentalism gives basic information as

well as opens perusers to a great many strategies and approaches utilized by prepared mentalists.

2. **Online Courses:** In the computerized age, online courses have become progressively famous for mastering new abilities, and clairvoyance is no special case. There are various internet-based stages that proposition seminars on mentalism, giving bit-by-bit direction on various methods and activities to upgrade one's clairvoyance powers. These courses frequently incorporate video instructional exercises, practice works, and intuitive tests to help students in their excursion of becoming capable in the specialty of telepathy.

3. **Studios and Courses:** Going to studios and courses directed by experienced mentalists can end up being a priceless asset for hopeful telepaths. These occasions give a stage to gaining from specialists in the field, who share their insight, bits of knowledge, and useful hints. In addition, these events frequently provide networking opportunities, opening doors for mentorship and collaboration with other enthusiasts and professionals.

4. **Props and Devices:** Mind perusing frequently depends on the utilization of props and devices to upgrade the presentation and make a more vivid encounter for the crowd. Probably the most normally utilized props incorporate playing a card game, pendulums, blindfolds, and books. These props are in many cases used in the execution of mentalist stunts and schedules to make an emanation of secret and wonder. Even

though the props themselves cannot read minds, they help the mentalist perform their tricks.

5. **Applications and Programming:** In the present innovation-driven world, there is a variety of applications and programming accessible that case to support mind perusing. These devices frequently influence the force of computerized reasoning, AI, and information examination to break down and decipher designs in the human way of behaving and language. While these devices may not give mystic capacities, they can help with social affairs and investigating data, empowering the mentalist to make precise forecasts or allowances.

6. **Practice and Experience:** At last, the way to turning into a talented telepath lies practically speaking and experience. No measure of books, courses, or apparatuses can supplant the significance of improving one's abilities through committed practice. Mentalism is a form of art that necessitates discipline, perseverance, and patience. By persistently rehearsing and acting before live crowds, hopeful telepaths can refine their strategies, gain from their slip-ups, and foster an instinctive feeling of guessing individuals' thoughts.

Mind perusing is an entrancing expertise that can be obtained by anybody able to contribute time and exertion. With the right apparatuses and assets, like books, online courses, studios, props, applications, and programming, people can dive into the universe of mentalism and investigate the specialty of telepathy.

Keep in mind, the way to dominance is long and requires practice and experience, however, the compensations of having the option to spellbind and amaze crowds with the force of the psyche make it all beneficial.

9.2. Suggest further telepathy devices

Mind-understanding instruments, otherwise called telepathy gadgets, have been a subject of interest for a long time. While the idea might appear as though something out of sci-fi, late headways in innovation have made it conceivable to investigate the fascinating universe of clairvoyance. These devices permit people to take advantage of the contemplations of others, opening up vast opportunities for correspondence, understanding, and self-improvement.

Assuming you are interested in mind perusing and might want to dig further into this captivating field, here are some suggested further telepathy instruments:

1. **Electroencephalography (EEG) Headsets**: EEG is a painless strategy that actions electrical action in the mind. EEG headsets can be worn on the scalp and are fit for recognizing brainwaves related to various mental states, feelings, and even goals. These headsets can be associated with different programming programs that break down the brainwave information and make an

interpretation of it into significant data. They can assist you with grasping your contemplations and feelings, as well as give a window into the personalities of others.

2. **fMRI, or functional magnetic resonance imaging:** fMRI is a method that actions mind movement by distinguishing changes in the bloodstream. This apparatus can show which regions of the mind are dynamic during various mental cycles and might uncover explicit considerations or goals. While customary fMRI machines are enormous and costly, there are currently versatile forms accessible that can be utilized beyond research labs. These convenient fMRI gadgets offer an astonishing open door for investigating mind perusing in regular daily existence.

3. **Mind PC Connection points (BCIs):** BCIs lay out an immediate correspondence pathway between the cerebrum and an outer gadget, bypassing conventional techniques for correspondence like discourse or contact. These connection points can be utilized to control outside gadgets, similar to PCs or automated appendages, utilizing just the force of thought. High-level BCIs can likewise translate the expectations behind unambiguous cerebrum designs, empowering mind-understanding capacities. While BCIs are essentially utilized for clinical purposes, they hold huge potential for mind-understanding applications.

4. **Brain Disentangling Calculations:** These calculations use AI procedures to translate and decipher mind

action. By preparing enormous datasets of mind action, these calculations can figure out how to recognize explicit mental states, goals, or even individual contemplations. Brain unraveling calculations have shown guarantee in different applications, including mind-controlled prosthetics, neurofeedback preparation, and mind understanding examination.

5. **Augmented Reality Telepathy Encounters:** Augmented reality (VR) innovation is being utilized to make vivid encounters that recreate mind perusing. These encounters can give a brief look into what seeing the considerations and feelings of others is like. VR mind-reading experiences allow users to investigate the ethical ramifications and difficulties of mind-reading in a controlled and secure setting, frequently involving simulated telepathy.

It is essential to keep in mind that, despite the significant advancements made in mind reading tools, their use is still fraught with ethical issues. Security, assent, and the potential for abuse are significant elements that should be addressed as clairvoyance innovation keeps on creating. Using mind-reading tools, you can learn about the mysteries of the human mind. There are a variety of recommended additional tools that can be used to delve deeper into the world of mind reading. These tools range from EEG headsets to fMRI machines, BCIs, neural decoding algorithms, and virtual reality experiences. As innovation progresses, these apparatuses will keep on advancing, possibly upsetting how we convey, comprehend, and interface with each other.

9. 3. Activities and exercises to upgrade your telepathy abilities

Mind perusing is the captivating skill of seeing another person's considerations and feelings with next to no verbal or actual correspondence. While it might appear as though a superpower held for the domain of sci-fi, some activities and exercises can assist with improving your telepathy abilities. By rehearsing these methods, you might have the option to foster a more profound comprehension of others and further develop your general relational abilities.

1. **Begin by rehearsing undivided attention:** Undivided attention includes completely zeroing in on the individual you are speaking with, focusing on their words, tone, and non-verbal communication. By effectively tuning in, you can start to get on unpretentious prompts and signals that uncover their actual contemplations and feelings. Practice undivided attention in your ordinary discussions, and put forth a cognizant attempt to figure out the other individual on a more profound level.

2. **Notice non-verbal communication:** Non-verbal communication plays a huge part in non-verbal correspondence. Focus on individuals' stances, looks, signals, and eye developments. These inconspicuous prompts can give experiences into their viewpoints and feelings. For example, crossed arms might show

preventiveness or conflict, while staying away from eye-to-eye connection might recommend uneasiness or misleading. The more you work on seeing non-verbal correspondence, the more you will need to decipher the certain messages people are passing on.

3. **Practice empathy:** The ability to comprehend and discuss another person's thoughts is empathy. Overhaul your clairvoyance capacities, is influential for making sympathy. Put yourself in the shoes of the singular you are associating with and endeavor to sort out their perspective. By empathizing with others, you can gain a deeper understanding of their thoughts and feelings, making it easier to precisely interpret their nonverbal cues.

4. **Upgrade your instinct:** Instinct is frequently alluded to as our "intuition," and it very well may be an incredible asset as a primary concern. To work on your instinct, practice contemplation and care works out. You will be able to tune into your intuition more effectively and develop a stronger sense of self-awareness with the assistance of these practices. Paying attention to your instinct senses can prompt a superior comprehension of others' viewpoints and feelings.

5. **Play speculating games**: Participating as a top priority in understanding games or exercises can be a tomfoolery and intelligent method for upgrading your capacities. For instance, take a stab at playing "20 Inquiries" with a companion, where you need to think about what item, individual, or situation they are

considering by requesting a series of yes-or-no inquiries. This game can assist you with refining your scrutinizing procedures and calibrating your capacity to get on unobtrusive clues.

6. **Concentrate on microexpressions:** Microexpressions are brief looks that keep going for a negligible portion of a second. They frequently reveal genuine feelings that people consciously or unconsciously try to hide. You can improve your ability to spot subtle emotional cues by studying microexpressions. You can learn how to recognize and interpret microexpressions by utilizing a variety of available resources, including books and online training programs.

7. **Take part in dynamic creative mind works out:** Dynamic creative mind practices include picturing and envisioning situations for you. Consider a loved one as an example, and then try to guess how they are feeling right now. Focus on the impressions and vibes that emerge to you. This exercise can assist with reinforcing your capacity to peruse individuals' considerations and feelings.

8. **Look for criticism and practice with others:** Practice and receiving feedback is one of the best ways to improve your mind-reading abilities. Take part in discussions with companions or relatives and request that they give legit criticism on your capacity to figure out their viewpoints and feelings. This permits you to refine your strategies and comprehend regions where you might have to get to the next level.

With hard work and practice, one can improve their mind-reading abilities over time. By integrating these activities and exercises into your day-to-day practice, you can upgrade your capacity to peruse individuals' considerations and feelings, prompting further developed correspondence and more grounded connections. Make sure to move toward mind perusing as an instrument for understanding and sympathy, as opposed to a method for control or control.

CONCLUSION

All through your telepathy process, you have without a doubt experienced different difficulties and wins. Reflecting upon this excursion permits you to acquire a more profound comprehension of yourself and your general surroundings.

Mind perusing is an expertise that requires tolerance and diligence. Understanding another person's thoughts and feelings necessitates the ability to observe and interpret both verbal and nonverbal cues. As you ponder your excursion, consider how far you have come from when you initially began. Recall the minutes where you battled and the minutes where you succeeded. These reflections will act as a wake up call of the headway you have made and the development you have encountered. It is essential to recognize that clairvoyance is definitely not a careful science. Essentially a device can help with better figuring out others. Pondering your encounters will assist you with perceiving the restrictions of clairvoyance and the significance of depending on different types of correspondence to acquire a total comprehension of an individual.

During your appearance, consider the techniques you have utilized to upgrade your clairvoyance abilities. Have you drilled undivided attention? Have you zeroed in on further developing your non-verbal relational abilities? Have you carved out opportunity to comprehend the social setting that might impact somebody's way of behaving? By looking at these systems, you can distinguish regions for development and foster new methods to additional improve your telepathy powers.

Techniques for mind reading can be used anywhere. They can be utilized in a variety of areas of your life to enhance your understanding of others and improve communication. By integrating these strategies into your everyday communications, you can develop more grounded connections and foster a more noteworthy feeling of compassion.

One viable utilization of telepathy strategies is in private connections. Whether it is with your better half, relatives, or companions, understanding their considerations and feelings can fundamentally reinforce your security. By effectively standing by listening to their words and focusing on their non-verbal communication, you can acquire further experiences into their sentiments and requirements. This can assist you with offering the help they require and work with additional significant associations.

Professional settings can also benefit from mind reading skills. Figuring out the contemplations and feelings of your partners, clients, or clients can work on your capacity to team up, arrange, and offer remarkable assistance. By perceiving their necessities and inspirations, you can tailor your way to deal with line up with their assumptions, making the communication more useful and fulfilling for all gatherings included.

Also, mind perusing can be applied to self-reflection. By turning out to be more receptive to your own considerations and feelings, you can all the more likely figure out your inspirations, wants, and triggers. You are able to take proactive steps toward your own growth and development and make decisions based on accurate information when you are self-aware.

Understanding human way of behaving is an integral asset that can decidedly influence numerous parts of your life. By embracing this power, you can foster a more noteworthy feeling of compassion, further develop your relational abilities, and upgrade your own and proficient connections. One of the vital advantages of understanding human way of behaving is the capacity to identify with others. Sympathy permits you to imagine another person's perspective and really figure out their point of view. This empowers you to answer in a more empathetic and steady way, encouraging more grounded associations and settling clashes all the more successfully.

Understanding human behavior can also help you communicate better. By perceiving specific examples of conduct, you can change your correspondence style to all the more likely impact others. For instance, assuming somebody seems restless or overpowered, you can adjust your correspondence to be really consoling and quieting. Thusly, you establish a more favorable climate for successful correspondence and understanding.

One more benefit of understanding human way of behaving is the capacity to foster better and additional satisfying connections. By noticing and deciphering the ways of behaving and feelings of people around you, you can recognize their necessities, wants, and limits. This permits you to explore associations with more noteworthy awareness and regard, bringing about more profound associations and expanded fulfillment for all gatherings included.

Considering your telepathy process gives important bits of

knowledge into your development and progress. Improved communication and comprehension in personal and professional relationships are made possible by incorporating mind reading techniques into your daily life. Empathy, improved communication, and more satisfying relationships are all made possible by accepting the power of understanding human behavior.

www.ingramcontent.com/pod-product-compliance
Lightning Source LLC
Chambersburg PA
CBHW060943260726
48661CB00005B/1742